Discover herStory

T J Akers

Ready to meet the amazing women who changed the world? The **herStory** series invites you on an incredible journey through time, told directly by the inspiring women themselves! Imagine stepping into their shoes, seeing the world through their eyes, and feeling their courage and passion.

From brave leaders and brilliant scientists to groundbreaking artists and powerful activists, each book in **herStory** brings a legendary woman to life in her own words. You'll learn about their dreams, challenges, and incredible achievements, discovering what made them truly special. These aren't just stories from the past; they're blueprints for your future!

Get ready to be inspired to dream big, be brave, and find your own powerful voice. Because every girl has a story worth telling, and it all starts with **herStory**!

This is a work of non-fiction. While based on historical events and figures, some dialogue and descriptive elements have been imagined for narrative purposes to engage young readers.

ISBN: 9798298076982

Printed in UK

Disclaimer: This book is intended for educational and inspirational purposes for young readers aged 8-13. While every effort has been made to ensure historical accuracy, it is a simplified narrative of complex events.

herStory: Ellie Goldstein

T J Akers

Introduction: A Sparkle in the Fashion World

Imagine a world where everyone is celebrated for who they are, where differences are seen as strengths, and where dreams, no matter how big or small, are within reach. This is the world that

Ellie Goldstein is helping to build, one stunning photograph and one joyful smile at a time. Ellie's journey is not just about fashion; it's about courage, determination, and the power of believing in yourself.

Born in Ilford, East London, Ellie entered the world with a sparkle that was destined to shine. Like many children, she had dreams, but perhaps some of the paths she would take were not those typically imagined for someone with Down syndrome. Yet, from a young age, Ellie showed an incredible spirit, a vibrant personality, and a natural ability to light up any room she entered. Her family fostered an environment of love and encouragement, always supporting her to explore her passions and embrace every opportunity. They saw her unique abilities, her infectious positivity, and her radiant confidence, and they knew she was capable of remarkable things.

Ellie's story is a modern "Her-story" because it challenges old ideas and opens up new possibilities. For a long time, the fashion world, with its glossy magazines and towering runways, often presented a very narrow idea of beauty. It seemed to say that only certain people, with certain looks, could be models. But Ellie, with her bright eyes, confident pose, and genuine happiness, has stepped onto that very stage and shown everyone that beauty comes in countless forms. She's not just a model; she's a trailblazer, breaking down barriers and proving that true beauty is about inner strength, joy, and authenticity.

Her journey into the spotlight began with a passion for performing and a natural flair in front of the camera. She joined a special agency that champions models with disabilities, helping them find their voice and showcase their talents. It was here that her potential truly began to blossom.

Each photoshoot, each new project, was a step forward, not just for Ellie, but for everyone who longs to see a more inclusive world. She has graced campaigns for huge global brands, her face beaming from billboards and social media feeds, sending a powerful message of diversity and acceptance.

Ellie's life, much like Queen Elizabeth II's, demonstrates the profound impact one person can have through their unwavering commitment to their unique purpose. While Queen Elizabeth's duty was to a nation and its Commonwealth, Ellie's duty is to a generation, to show them that every single person has value and can achieve incredible things. She teaches us about the importance of self-love, about embracing what makes us different, and about speaking up for what is right. She embodies resilience, not just in facing challenges, but in joyfully celebrating her true self in a world that sometimes struggles to understand.

For young girls, Ellie Goldstein's life offers inspiring lessons. It shows that your uniqueness is your superpower. It teaches us to be brave enough to be ourselves, even when it feels like we don't fit in. It highlights the importance of pursuing your passions and finding communities that support you. And perhaps most importantly, it reminds us that true strength lies in kindness, inclusivity, and the belief that every story is worth telling, especially your own. In the chapters that follow, we will journey through Ellie's vibrant life, discovering her early passions, her first steps into the modelling world, and the powerful impact she is making, encouraging all of us to shine brightly.

Chapter 1: My Early Sparkle

Hello there! My name is Ellie, and this is my story. Not just any story, but *my* story, about how I found my voice, my confidence, and my way to shine in a world that's always learning to be a little bit brighter. I was born in Ilford, a busy part of East

London, and from the very beginning, I think I brought a lot of sparkle with me! My family always tells me I was a happy baby, full of giggles and ready to explore everything around me.

Growing up, my home was always filled with love and laughter. My mum, dad, and sister were (and still are!) my biggest cheerleaders. They saw me, really saw me, for who I was – a bright, curious, and energetic girl who loved to have fun. I have Down syndrome, and sometimes people might have certain ideas about what that means. But for my family, it just meant I was *me*, Ellie, with all my wonderful qualities. They never let anything limit what they believed I could do, and that made all the difference. My mum, Yvonne, always says I was a little ray of sunshine from the moment I arrived. She remembers my big, curious eyes taking everything in, and my infectious giggle that could make anyone smile. My dad, Mark, was always the one to encourage my adventurous side, cheering me on when I tried new things. And my sister, Amy, was my first best friend, my partner in crime for all our childhood games and imaginary adventures. We're still super close, and I love spending time with her.

I remember my early childhood being full of exciting discoveries. Our house in Ilford felt like a world of wonder. I loved playing games, drawing colourful pictures, and listening to music. Music always made me want to move! I loved to dance and pretend to be a pop star. I wasn't shy about expressing myself, and if there was a stage, even a pretend one in our living room, I was ready to perform! My sister and I would put on shows for our parents, singing and dancing until we were out of breath. These were some of my favourite times, just being free and joyful. I especially loved pop music, and I'd spend hours mimicking my favourite singers, using a hairbrush as a microphone, belting out songs with all my heart.

My parents would clap and cheer, and sometimes even join in, turning our living room into a lively concert hall. These moments, filled with music and laughter, were so important because they taught me that it was okay, even wonderful, to be expressive and a little bit loud sometimes!

I vividly remember the textures and colours around our home. The soft carpet where I'd spend hours playing with my toys, the bright sunshine streaming through the windows, and the delicious smells of my mum's cooking filling the kitchen. Simple things like building tall towers with blocks, playing hide-and-seek with Amy, or splashing in puddles after a rain shower felt like the biggest adventures. I was a very tactile child, loving to touch and explore everything. I loved the feel of soft blankets, the cool smoothness of a polished wooden table, and the sensation of digging my hands into sand at the park. Each new sensation was a small joy, a part of how I understood the world.

When I started school, it was a big change, but also very exciting. I loved learning new things and making wonderful friends. I remember my teachers being very kind and patient, always helping me understand things in a way that made sense to me. Learning to read and write was a big adventure, like unlocking a secret code that opened up a whole world of stories. I loved books that were full of pictures and exciting characters, especially those about strong girls who went on adventures. Reading felt like a superpower because it allowed me to imagine so many different lives and possibilities. My favorite subjects were anything creative – art, music, and drama. These were the lessons where I felt most at ease, where I could truly let my imagination soar.

Being with my friends was so much fun – we'd laugh, share secrets, and play games during break time. We'd play tag, or swing as high as we could on the playground, feeling the wind in our hair. I also loved quieter games, like drawing together or sharing our favourite snacks. It was important to me to feel like I belonged, and my friends always made me feel like I was a valued part of our group. They saw me for me, not for my Down syndrome. We were just kids, enjoying each other's company. I learned that having good friends by your side makes everything better, especially when you're trying new things or facing a challenge. My family always taught me to be kind, to listen to others, and to always try to see the good in people. These lessons helped me build strong friendships that I still cherish today. I remember one time, when I was struggling with a tricky math problem, my friend Sarah stayed with me during playtime to help me figure it out. That small act of kindness meant so much to me, showing me the true value of friendship.

I also discovered a love for performing early on. It started with those living room concerts, but then I got involved in school plays and local drama groups. There was something magical about being on stage, feeling the spotlights on my face, and seeing the audience smile or clap. It gave me a special feeling inside, a kind of energy that just made me want to do it more. I loved the process of rehearsing, learning lines, and becoming a different character. One time, in a school play about jungle animals, I was a very proud lion. I remember roaring loudly and making all my friends laugh! The applause at the end of the show felt like pure magic. This experience, even in its simplest form, showed me that I enjoyed being watched, that I liked entertaining people, and that I felt confident when I was performing. I think that's where the seed of wanting to be a model or an actress first started to grow, even if I didn't quite know it yet.

My parents encouraged all my interests, from dancing to painting, because they wanted me to find what made me happy and what made my heart sing. They understood that everyone has their own unique talents and passions, and it's important to nurture them. They never pushed me, but they always opened doors. If I said I wanted to try something, they would find a way to make it happen. This freedom to explore, to try things without fear of failure, was a huge gift. It taught me that it's okay to experiment, to find what lights you up, and to celebrate every small victory along the way. They often told me, "Ellie, you can do anything you set your mind to," and I really believed them. That belief, coming from them, became a powerful voice inside my own head.

One specific memory that stands out from my early years is a trip to the beach. I loved the feeling of the sand between my toes and the cool water splashing against my legs. I remember building a huge sandcastle with Amy, decorating it with shells we found. The waves would come in and wash parts of it away, and at first, I'd be a little sad. But then my dad would say, "Time to build it even stronger, Ellie!" And we'd laugh and start all over again. That simple experience taught me a quiet lesson about resilience – that sometimes things don't go perfectly, but you can always try again, and often, you can build something even better.

My childhood was also filled with everyday routines that, looking back, provided such comfort and stability. Family dinners where we'd all talk about our day, bedtime stories read by my mum or dad, and weekend trips to the park or museum. These small moments built a strong foundation of love and security. They taught me the importance of family bonds, of listening to each other, and of just being present. My family always made sure I felt loved and safe, and that gave me the confidence to explore the world around me. They also taught me about my Down syndrome in a very natural way. It wasn't something to hide or be ashamed of; it was just a part of who I was, like my brown hair or my love for bright colours. They showed me that my abilities were what mattered, and that I was capable of so much.

In this chapter, I've tried to take you back to those early days, sharing my memories of growing up, the games I played, the friends I made, and the moments that helped me discover the bright, confident person I was becoming. It's about finding your own spark, understanding that you are special just the way you are, and knowing that your unique qualities are what make you beautiful. It's about those first glimmers of knowing who you are and what you love, surrounded by the warmth of family and friendship. Every laugh, every new skill learned, every moment of imaginative play, was a step on the path to becoming the Ellie I am today. And it all started with that early sparkle, right here in Ilford.

Chapter 2: Discovering My Voice

As I grew a little older, I started to think more about what I really loved to do and what made me feel alive. Performing was definitely one of those things. I loved being in front of the camera, or on a stage, feeling that excitement build up inside me. My family noticed this too, and they were always looking for ways to help me explore my interests. They believed that everyone deserves a chance to follow their dreams, and they wanted to make sure I had every opportunity.

One day, my mum and I were talking about how much I loved drama and being in plays. She mentioned that there were special agencies that worked with models and actors who had disabilities, and how they helped people like me find opportunities to show the world our talents. I remember my eyes widening! It sounded like something out of a dream. It felt like a door was opening to a whole new world, a world where I could truly be myself and express my creativity in a way I hadn't imagined before. I was a little nervous, because it was something new and a bit different from anything I'd done before, but I was mostly excited. The idea of seeing myself in pictures, like the models I sometimes saw in magazines, was thrilling.

That's how we found Zebedee Management. They are an amazing team who believe in celebrating diversity and showing that beauty comes in all shapes, sizes, and abilities. From the very first phone call and email, I felt so welcomed and understood. It wasn't just a business; it felt like a family. When I first met them in person, they didn't see me as "Ellie with Down syndrome"; they saw me as "Ellie, the talented and confident model." That feeling of being seen for my potential, rather than any perceived limitations, was incredibly empowering. They asked me about my hobbies, my favourite music, and what made me happy. They truly wanted to get to know the real me, not just a model profile.

Joining Zebedee Management was a huge step, like stepping onto a new, exciting path. They began to teach me about modelling, which was much more than just standing still and smiling. They taught me about posing – how to hold my body to show off the clothes, how to use my hands, and where to look. They explained how to use my expressions to tell a story without words. Sometimes a picture needs to look happy, sometimes thoughtful, sometimes strong. It wasn't just about looking pretty; it was about communicating, about showing personality and emotion through my face and body. I learned that my eyes could tell a whole story just by themselves!

My first photoshoots were a big learning experience. It was quite different from just playing dress-up at home! Suddenly, there were bright lights, huge cameras that clicked and whirred, and a whole team of people – photographers, stylists, makeup artists, and assistants. Everyone was so professional, but also very kind and encouraging. I remember feeling a bit shy at first, a little overwhelmed by all the equipment and the busy atmosphere. My mum was often there with me, which helped a lot. She would give me a reassuring smile or a quick whisper of encouragement, and that always made me feel more confident.

I remember one of my very first shoots. It was a test shoot, which is when a model works with a photographer to practice and build their portfolio. We were in a studio, and it was a bit chilly, but the clothes were colourful and fun. The photographer, a kind lady with a gentle voice, showed me how to stand, how to turn my head slightly, and how to relax my shoulders. At first, it felt a bit stiff, like my body wasn't quite doing what I wanted it to do. My smile felt a bit forced. But she was so patient. She'd say, "Ellie, imagine your favourite song is playing! How would you move?" Or, "Think about something that makes you really happy!" And just like that, the stiffness would melt away, and my natural smile would appear. It was like magic!

I learned that communication on a photoshoot is very important. The photographer might give directions like, "Chin up a little," or "Softer eyes," or "Give me some movement." It was like learning a new language, the language of the camera. I focused hard, trying to understand exactly what they wanted. I also learned that it was okay to ask questions if I didn't understand something. Everyone was there to help me do my best. The stylists would bring amazing clothes – sometimes bright and colourful, sometimes elegant and flowing. I loved trying on different outfits and seeing how they changed my look and how I felt. And the makeup artists! They were so clever, making my eyes sparkle even more and making my skin look smooth and radiant. It truly felt like being transformed into a character for a few hours.

The biggest difference between pretending to be a pop star at home and being a professional model was the focus. At home, it was just for fun. On a set, it was about creating a specific image for a brand, and there were lots of people working together to make that happen. There was a schedule, and everyone had a job to do. But even with all that professionalism, the core feeling was still joy. I was doing something I loved, and I was helping to create something beautiful. It was exciting to see how all the different parts of the team worked together, like a well-oiled machine, to make the magic happen.

After those first few test shoots, I started getting small jobs. Maybe for a local boutique, or for an online catalogue. Each one was a step forward, helping me gain more experience and confidence. I learned to relax more in front of the camera, to trust my instincts, and to let my personality shine through. It wasn't always perfect, of course. Sometimes a pose felt awkward, or my smile didn't quite look right. But I learned that mistakes are just opportunities to learn, and every photoshoot, whether big or small, taught me something new. The teams I worked with were always encouraging, reminding me that it was okay to be myself and to have fun. That encouragement was like fuel for my confidence.

As I started to see my pictures appear in different places, even small ones, a new feeling began to grow inside me. It wasn't just about my own journey anymore. I realized that by simply being myself, by being confident and happy in front of the camera, I was showing the world something important. I was showing that people with Down syndrome *can* be models, that we *can* be beautiful, and that we *can* be visible in the fashion world. It felt like I was breaking down tiny walls, brick by brick, just by being me. That realization made me even more determined to keep going. I wanted to show every young girl out there that if you have a dream and you work hard, you can make it happen, no matter what challenges you might face.

I found my own unique way to shine. It's about discovering your talents and finding the courage to pursue them, even when they seem a little out of reach. It's also about finding people who believe in you and help you make your dreams come true, and the incredible feeling of knowing that your unique presence can help change the world for the better.

Chapter 3: My First Big Break!

Every model dreams of that one big job, the one that makes everyone sit up and take notice. For me, that moment arrived in 2020, and it felt like a real fairytale! I was chosen to be part of a campaign for Gucci Beauty, one of the biggest and most famous fashion brands in the world. Can you imagine? Little me, from Ilford, modelling for Gucci!

The phone call from my agent, Laura, from Zebedee Management, felt different from any other. I remember it was a regular afternoon, and Mum was with me. When Laura told us it was for Gucci, my jaw nearly dropped! I think I actually squealed with excitement. Mum looked at me with this huge, proud smile, and we hugged each other tight. It felt surreal, like a dream that was suddenly coming true. We talked about it for hours that day, calling my dad and sister to share the amazing news. It was the kind of news that makes your heart beat a little faster and your mind race with possibilities. A campaign for a brand like Gucci wasn't just a big job; it was a statement. It was a sign that the fashion world was truly beginning to open its eyes to beauty in all its forms.

The campaign was for a new mascara, and it was a special project called #GucciBeautyGlossyMascara. The idea behind it was beautiful: to celebrate different kinds of beauty, to show that everyone is beautiful in their own way, and that makeup is for enhancing who you are, not changing it. And that's exactly what I believe! It felt like the perfect message for me to be a part of. The brief from Gucci emphasized authenticity and joy, which are two things I love to bring to everything I do.

Preparing for the shoot was a mix of excitement and a tiny bit of nerves. My mum and I discussed what it would be like, based on the information Zebedee gave us. We knew it would be a professional set, with lots of people, but Zebedee always makes sure their models feel comfortable and supported. I spent some time practicing my poses in front of the mirror, thinking about different expressions – happy, thoughtful, strong. I wanted to be ready to give my absolute best. I also spent extra time practicing my 'mascara face' – that little open-mouthed look you sometimes do when you're putting on mascara! It seemed funny, but I knew it was important for the product.

When the day of the shoot arrived, I woke up feeling a buzz of energy. The studio was in London, and it was a large, bright space, filled with activity. There were huge lights on stands, cameras with big lenses, and racks of clothes – though for a beauty campaign, the focus was mostly on my face! The team at Gucci was amazing. From the moment I walked in, I felt so welcomed. Everyone was smiling, friendly, and made me feel like a true professional. There was a lovely warmth about the atmosphere, not at all what I had imagined from such a big, famous brand.

I met the photographer, David PD Hyde. He had a very kind and calm presence, and he immediately made me feel at ease. He talked to me, not just about the pictures, but about my interests, my family, and what made me happy. This helped me to relax and feel natural. He explained what we were going to do and showed me some examples of the kind of looks they wanted.

Then it was time for hair and makeup! This is always one of my favourite parts of a shoot. The makeup artist had so many brushes and palettes, like an artist with their paints. They were so gentle and skilled, making my eyes sparkle even more and highlighting my features. I remember them applying the mascara – that very mascara I was there to promote! – and explaining how it worked. It felt special to be part of bringing a product to life. They also did my hair, making it look styled but still natural, complementing the overall look. It truly felt like being transformed into a character for a few hours, a super confident and glamorous version of myself.

Once hair and makeup were done, it was time to step in front of the camera. The lights were bright, but I focused on David, the photographer. He was great at giving directions, like "Ellie, can you tilt your head slightly?" or "Look into the lens, that's it, beautiful!" He played music, which always helps me relax and get into a rhythm. I remember trying different poses, some standing, some sitting, focusing on my eyes and hands to convey the right feeling. We took lots and lots of pictures, exploring different angles and expressions. Sometimes I'd feel silly, but David would always laugh with me and say, "Perfect, Ellie, exactly what we need!" His encouragement was invaluable.

It was a really long day, stretching for many hours, but every minute was exciting. There were breaks for snacks and drinks, and the team would chat with me, making sure I was comfortable and not too tired. I loved seeing the little screens where

David would show me some of the shots he was taking. It was amazing to see how the lights and the camera captured something special. I could see the vision coming to life, and it filled me with a sense of accomplishment. I felt like I was truly contributing, not just standing there, but actively participating in the creative process.

When the photos were finally released, they went everywhere! It felt like my face was suddenly all over the internet. My picture was on Gucci's social media accounts, which have millions of followers. It was in fashion magazines, online news articles, and blogs all over the world. My friends and family were absolutely over the moon. My sister, Amy, kept sending me screenshots from her phone, saying, "Ellie, look! You're everywhere!" My mum cried happy tears, and my dad puffed out his chest with pride. It was incredible to see how far my image travelled, from a studio in London to screens and pages across continents.

That's when I truly realised this wasn't just a job for me; it was something much, much bigger. My pictures were helping to change how people thought about beauty and who could be a model. I started getting messages from people I didn't even know, from all over the world, saying how much my photos inspired them. Parents of children with Down syndrome wrote to my agency, expressing their joy and gratitude for seeing someone like me represented. Young girls told me that seeing my photos made them feel more confident about themselves. These messages were the most rewarding part of the whole experience. They made my heart swell with happiness and a deep sense of purpose.

The reaction was mostly wonderful, with so many positive comments and people celebrating diversity. It felt like a wave of positive energy. Of course, sometimes, when you put yourself out there, there can be some unkind comments too.

The internet can be a place where people say things without thinking, and some people might not understand or accept differences. It used to make me a little sad at first, seeing a negative comment. But I quickly learned to focus on the love and support. My family always taught me to be strong and to believe in myself, and that helped me remember that my worth isn't defined by what a few people might say. They reminded me that for every negative comment, there were hundreds, even thousands, of positive ones. The positive messages truly outweighed any negativity, and they made me feel so proud of what I was achieving, and proud to be myself. I understood that my job wasn't to change the minds of everyone, but to be a light for those who needed to see it.

The Gucci campaign wasn't just a moment in time; it opened doors and started conversations. It showed that inclusivity wasn't just a trend, but a vital and beautiful part of the future of fashion. It paved the way for more models with disabilities to be seen and celebrated, creating more opportunities for people like me. It made me feel like I was part of something truly significant, a movement towards a more accepting and diverse world. And it all started with one incredible opportunity, one big break that changed everything.

Chapter 4: More Brands, More Smiles

After the Gucci campaign, it felt like the floodgates opened! More brands wanted to work with me, and I was so excited to take on new projects. It proved that my first big break wasn't just a one-off; it was a sign that the fashion world was slowly but surely opening its arms to more diverse faces. Each new job was an adventure, a chance to work with different creative teams and show different sides of myself.

I've had the amazing opportunity to model for other fantastic brands like Adidas, Superdrug, and Disney. Every single one was a unique experience. With Adidas, it was all about movement and feeling strong and athletic. I loved wearing their cool sportswear and showing that activewear is for everyone. For Superdrug, a big beauty and health store, I got to show my natural smile and promote products that help people feel good about themselves. And Disney... well, who doesn't love Disney?! Being part of a Disney campaign felt like being part of something truly magical, connecting with characters and stories that bring joy to so many.

Let me tell you about the Adidas experience first. This was a really exciting one for me because I love to be active and to dance. When my agent told me Adidas was interested, I immediately thought about all the cool trainers and sportswear. The brief for this campaign was about showing authenticity and everyday activity. They wanted to feature real people, doing real things, which felt very natural for me.

The shoot itself was different from the Gucci one. While Gucci was about beauty and expressive faces, Adidas was much more about movement and dynamic poses. We shot in a studio, but also sometimes outside, pretending to be running or stretching. The clothes were amazing – super comfortable and colourful trainers, leggings, and hoodies. I loved wearing them because they made me feel sporty and ready for anything! The photographer was great at encouraging me to jump, stretch, and move naturally. Sometimes I'd feel a bit tired, but the energy on set was always high. We'd listen to upbeat music, and the team would cheer me on. I learned to use my whole body to express energy and confidence. It wasn't just about looking at the camera; it was about embodying the feeling of being active and strong. I remember one shot where I had to pretend to be mid-jump, and it took a few tries to get it just right, but when we did, everyone clapped. That sense of accomplishment was fantastic.

When the Adidas campaign came out, it felt amazing to see my photos everywhere, especially in places like sports shops or online ads for sportswear. It sent such a powerful message: that activewear is for everyone, no matter your ability. It wasn't just about professional athletes; it was about enjoying movement and feeling good in your own skin. I felt really proud to be part of that message, showing that fitness and style are for all bodies. It sparked conversations about adaptive clothing and inclusive fitness, which is so important.

Next came the campaign for Superdrug. This was a different kind of beauty brand from Gucci. Superdrug is a high street store, so it's about everyday beauty products, things that everyone uses. This campaign felt very real and relatable. They wanted to show a natural, friendly, and accessible kind of beauty.

The shoot for Superdrug was focused on showing a fresh, happy look. I modelled makeup products, but also skincare and hair products. The atmosphere was very relaxed and friendly, almost like hanging out with friends. The makeup artists and hairstylists focused on enhancing my natural features, rather than creating a dramatic look. They used bright, friendly colours and made sure my skin looked glowing. I loved trying out different lip glosses and eyeshadows! We also did some shots with hair products, showing off healthy, shiny hair. It was all about feeling good and confident in your own skin, which is a message I truly believe in.

What I loved about the Superdrug campaign was its accessibility. Seeing my face in a store that so many people visit every day felt very impactful. It showed that everyone, regardless of their background or abilities, deserves to feel beautiful and to have access to products that make them feel good. It was about everyday confidence and the joy of self-care. I remember seeing my picture in a Superdrug store window for the first time, and it made me smile from ear to ear. It felt like I was directly connecting with people in their daily lives.

And then, there was Disney! Oh, my goodness, this was truly a dream come true. Who doesn't love Disney?! From when I was a little girl, I adored Disney movies – the princesses, the magic, the singing, the beautiful stories. Being part of a Disney campaign felt like stepping right into one of those fairytales. The excitement I felt for this one was different; it was pure childhood joy mixed with the thrill of professional work.

The Disney campaign was themed around celebrating imagination and inclusivity, bringing beloved characters to life in new ways. The sets were magical, with lots of bright colours and playful props. I got to wear some fantastic clothes that hinted at Disney themes, but still felt very stylish. I remember some outfits had subtle hints of classic characters, which was really fun to spot! The photographers and directors on this shoot were brilliant at encouraging playful expressions and natural smiles. They wanted to capture the wonder and joy that Disney brings to people. We played games on set to get natural reactions, and sometimes they'd play Disney songs, which helped me get into the mood! It truly felt like a big, joyful playdate, but with cameras rolling.

Being part of a Disney campaign felt special because Disney is a brand that reaches so many children around the world. Knowing that young girls, just like I was, would see me in a Disney ad, filled me with immense happiness. It reinforces the message that dreams really do come true, and that imagination and joy are for everyone. It shows that heroes and models come in all forms, and that every child deserves to see themselves reflected in the stories they love. This campaign felt like a direct link back to my own childhood dreams of performing and being part of something magical.

Each campaign comes with its own set of challenges and triumphs, of course. Sometimes the days are very long. I might have to wake up really early to travel to the studio, and then stay late to finish all the shots. There can be lots of waiting around while they change the lights or the set. Sometimes it's cold on set, especially if we're shooting outside in England! And sometimes, I have to hold a pose for a long time, which can make my muscles ache a bit. But I always try to remember why I'm doing it – to create beautiful images and send a positive message. I take breaks when I need them, I drink plenty of water, and I always try to keep my energy up. My mum is usually with me on set, and she's my absolute rock, making sure I'm comfortable and happy. She brings snacks and tells me jokes, and her presence always helps me stay focused and positive.

The energy of the team always helps too. Whether it's the photographer, the makeup artist, the stylist, or the assistants, everyone is working together, and their enthusiasm is contagious. I love meeting new people on these shoots. Everyone has a different story, and it's wonderful to learn from them. I've met so many creative and kind people who truly believe in what Zebedee and I are trying to achieve – making the fashion world more inclusive.

I also learn something new about myself with every job. With Adidas, I learned how to use my body more expressively. With Superdrug, I focused on a more natural, radiant beauty. And with Disney, it was all about capturing pure joy and imagination. Sometimes I discover a new favourite pose, or a way to express an emotion with just my eyes. Sometimes it's about pushing myself out of my comfort zone, like when I have to model something a bit unusual or try a new kind of expression! But it's always fun, and I always try to bring my positive energy to the set. I believe that if you enjoy what you're doing, it shows in your pictures. My genuine happiness really comes through, and I think that's why these campaigns have resonated with so many people.

Beyond these big brands, I've also had the pleasure of working on many other exciting projects – smaller fashion editorials, charity campaigns, and even some fun online collaborations. Each one is a valuable experience, helping me grow as a model and as a person. They all contribute to the bigger picture: showing that diversity is not just a trend, but the beautiful reality of our world. Every step, big or small, helps to make a difference and chip away at old-fashioned ideas about who can be a model. It's an amazing feeling to be part of this change.

Chapter 5: More Than Just a Model

Being a model is amazing, but my work is about so much more than just looking good in clothes. It's about sending a message, about changing minds, and about showing the world that people with Down syndrome, and all disabilities, are capable, beautiful, and valuable. I've become an advocate for inclusivity and diversity, and it's a role I take very seriously and one that fills me with immense pride.

After the Gucci campaign and other amazing opportunities, I realized that my face and my story were reaching so many people. It wasn't just about striking a pose or wearing beautiful clothes anymore; it was about the bigger picture. It was about using this amazing platform to make a real difference in the world. I found myself speaking out more and more, sharing my experiences in interviews, on social media, and sometimes even at events. This felt like a natural next step, a way to use my voice for good.

One of the most important things I want to show is that people with disabilities are capable, beautiful, and valuable. For a long time, people with disabilities weren't seen much in fashion, on TV, or in movies. It was almost like we were invisible. But we are here, and we have so much to offer! I want to break down those old ideas and show everyone how amazing and diverse the world truly is. When I speak about this, I often think about young girls, maybe a girl with Down syndrome just like me, who might be looking at a magazine or watching TV and wishing they could see someone who looks like them. I want to be that person for them. I want them to see me and think, "If Ellie can do it, so can I!" That thought makes my heart feel so full.

It's so important for everyone to see people who look like them, or who have similar experiences, being successful and celebrated. This is what we call representation. Imagine if all the books you read only had characters with blue eyes and blonde hair. If you had brown eyes and black hair, you might start to feel like you weren't important, or that your story wasn't worth telling. That's why representation is so crucial – it helps everyone feel seen, valued, and like they belong. I remember when I was younger, I didn't see many models like me in magazines or on TV. Now, I get to be that person for others, and that feels truly special. I hope my visibility helps open doors for even more diverse models in the future.

Another big message I love to talk about is the power of self-belief and self-love. It's so easy to compare yourself to others. You might look at someone on social media or in a magazine and think, "Oh, I wish I looked like that," or "I wish I could do that." But I've learned that the most important thing is to love yourself just as you are. My unique qualities, including having Down syndrome, are a part of what makes me *me*, and I wouldn't change them. They give me a unique perspective and a special way of connecting with people. My mum often tells me that my positive attitude and my natural happiness are gifts. Those are qualities that come from within me, and they are just as important as how I look in a photo.

Learning to love yourself means celebrating your strengths and accepting your weaknesses. It means being kind to yourself, even when you make mistakes. It means understanding that you are unique, and that's your superpower! I try to remind myself every day that I am capable and strong. If I ever feel a bit down or unsure, I think about all the things I've achieved and all the people who support me. I want to encourage everyone to embrace what makes them different, because those differences are what make you beautiful and unique. Don't try to be someone else; be the best version of *you*.

I also believe strongly in the power of kindness. The fashion industry, and the world in general, can be tough sometimes. There are busy schedules, high expectations, and sometimes, as

I mentioned before, unkind comments online. But I try to always be kind, to be polite, and to bring a positive attitude to every situation. I believe that being kind helps to build bridges between people and shows everyone that we are all in this together.

On set, I always try to say hello to everyone, from the photographer to the assistants who bring the water. A simple "thank you" or a smile can make a big difference to someone's day. I've learned that a positive attitude can spread like sunshine. If I'm happy and enthusiastic, it often makes the whole team feel more joyful and energized. When people are kind to me, it makes me feel strong and supported, and I want to pass that feeling on. It's like a chain reaction of goodness! Kindness isn't just about being nice; it's about showing respect and empathy for others. It makes the world a warmer and more welcoming place for everyone.

I've had opportunities to share my story in various interviews, and each time, I feel a sense of purpose. I remember one interview where a journalist asked me what advice I would give to other young people with Down syndrome who want to achieve their dreams. I told them: "Believe in yourself. Never give up on your dreams. And don't let anyone tell you that you can't do something." It was a simple message, but it came from my heart. I often think about that interview and hope my words reached someone who needed to hear them. I also use my social media to share positive messages, to post pictures that celebrate diversity, and to connect with my followers. It's a powerful way to share my message with a huge audience.

Being an advocate means using my platform to create a more understanding and accepting world. It means showing that beauty is truly diverse and that everyone deserves to be celebrated. It means challenging old ideas and pushing for new, exciting ones where everyone is included. This role fills me with immense pride because I know I am part of a larger movement that is making the world a better place for future generations. It's not always easy, but knowing that I am helping others gives me the strength and motivation to keep going. My goal is to keep shining my light brightly, so that others can see their own light too.

Chapter 6: My Passions Outside Modelling

Even though modelling is a huge part of my life and I absolutely love it, I have many other passions that bring me joy and keep me grounded. It's important to have hobbies and interests outside of your main work, things that let you relax, be creative, and just be yourself. For me, these passions often involve movement, creativity, and spending time with the people I love. They're like different ingredients that make up my happy recipe of life!

Dancing is one of my biggest passions! Remember how I used to pretend to be a pop star when I was little, using a hairbrush as a microphone? Well, that love for movement and music never went away. I love to dance to all kinds of music – pop, hip-hop, anything with a good beat. If a song comes on that I like, my feet just start tapping, and pretty soon, I'm moving! Dancing makes me feel free and happy, and it's a wonderful way to express myself without words. It's great exercise too, and I always feel energized after a good dance session.

I take dance classes, and that's a lot of fun. We learn different routines, and sometimes we even perform them. I love the feeling of moving in sync with others, and the challenge of learning new steps. My favorite is probably hip-hop because it has so much energy and you can really put your own style into it. But I also enjoy more gentle dances, where the movements are flowing and graceful. Even when I'm just at home, if a good song comes on, I'll have an impromptu dance party in the living room. My mum and sister often join in, and we just laugh and dance until we're out of breath. It's a wonderful way to shake off any worries and just feel pure joy. Dancing helps me connect with my body and my feelings, and it's a constant reminder of how much fun movement can be. It's also a way to be creative because you can tell a story with your body.

I also love to draw and be creative with art. I enjoy sketching with pencils, coloring with crayons, and even painting with bright acrylics. Bringing my ideas to life on paper is incredibly satisfying. Sometimes I draw things I see around me, like a vase of flowers, or my favorite corgi dog, or a beautiful sunset. Other times, I just let my imagination run wild and create something completely new – fantastical creatures, abstract shapes, or colourful patterns that make me happy. There's something very calming about sitting down with my art supplies and just letting my hands create. It's a way for me to unwind and just be in the moment, away from the busy world of photoshoots. I don't worry about whether my art is "perfect"; I just enjoy the process of making something beautiful and expressing myself. It's a quiet kind of happiness, different from the energy of dancing, but just as fulfilling. I love seeing the colours mix and blend, and watching a blank page slowly fill up with my own creations. Sometimes I even make little cards for my family and friends, drawing something special for them. It's wonderful to share my art with people I love.

Spending time with my family and friends is also incredibly important to me. They are my rock, my cheerleaders, and the people who know me best. We love to go on outings together. A favourite activity is going to the cinema to watch a new movie. We buy popcorn and drinks, and it's so exciting to sit in the dark and get lost in a story on the big screen. After the movie, we always talk about our favourite parts.

We also love going out for meals, trying different restaurants. Sometimes it's Italian food, sometimes Chinese, and I always love dessert! These meals are not just about the food, though; they're about sharing stories, laughing, and catching up on each other's day. It's those moments of connection, just being together, that are so precious.

When the weather is nice, we love to visit new places or go on adventures. A day trip to the beach is always a highlight. I love the feeling of the sand between my toes, collecting shells, and splashing in the waves. We often go for walks in the park, enjoying the fresh air and seeing the trees and flowers. Sometimes, we even visit museums or galleries, which is fascinating because you learn so much and see amazing historical items or beautiful art. Even when we're just sitting at home, watching a movie together, or playing a board game, these moments are precious. They remind me of the love and support that surrounds me every day, and they help me stay connected to the people who matter most. My sister, Amy, and I still love to bake together sometimes, making cookies or cakes. It's always a little bit messy, but so much fun!

My friends are also a huge part of my life. We like to go shopping together, trying on clothes and having fun. We also love getting together for sleepovers, watching movies, listening to music, and talking for hours. They understand me, and we share so many laughs and secrets. Having friends who support you and make you feel good is a true gift. We often just hang out, listening to music, gossiping, and making each other laugh. These are the moments where I can truly relax and just be myself, without any cameras or expectations. They remind me that even though my life has changed a lot, the simple joys of friendship are still the most important. We might go for walks, grab a coffee, or just spend an afternoon chatting and drawing. It's so nice to have people who you can be completely yourself around.

Beyond these main interests, I also enjoy other small hobbies that help me relax. I like doing puzzles, whether it's a jigsaw puzzle or a word search. It's a nice way to focus my mind and feel a sense of accomplishment when I finish one. I also enjoy listening to podcasts, especially ones that tell interesting stories or teach me new things. And I love reading! Getting lost in a good book is a wonderful escape.

These passions are so important because they help me find balance in my life. Modelling is exciting and wonderful, but it can also be very busy and demanding. Having these hobbies and spending time with my loved ones helps me relax, recharge, and remember who I am outside of the spotlight. They keep me grounded and remind me of the simple joys in life. They are moments just for me, or for me and the people I cherish, where I can just be Ellie, without thinking about poses or campaigns. It's about nourishing my spirit and taking care of my well-being, so I can continue to shine brightly in all areas of my life. These activities are what make me happy from the inside out, and that inner happiness is what truly makes me sparkle.

Chapter 7: Facing Challenges with a Smile

Life isn't always sunshine and photoshoots. Sometimes, just like everyone else, I face challenges. Being a model with Down syndrome means that sometimes I encounter misunderstandings or people who might not know how to interact with me. But I've learned to face these moments with courage, a positive attitude, and often, a big smile.

One of the biggest challenges I face, which might surprise you, is the sheer physical demand of modelling. It's not just standing there and looking pretty! Sometimes, a photoshoot can last all day, from early morning until late in the evening. This means waking up super early to travel to the studio, often before the sun is even up! Then, once I'm there, it's a lot of standing, posing, and repeating the same movements over and over until the photographer gets just the right shot. Imagine trying to hold a perfect smile or a tricky pose for a whole minute, and then doing it again, and again! My legs can get tired, my arms might ache, and sometimes my cheeks even hurt from smiling so much!

There's also a lot of waiting around on set. While the team changes the lighting, adjusts the props, or gets a new outfit ready, I might have to sit and wait. Patience is a skill I've definitely learned! My mum is usually with me, and she's a huge help. She makes sure I have snacks and water, and we might chat or listen to music to pass the time. Sometimes, I bring a book or my drawing pad to keep myself busy. It's important to stay focused, but also to save my energy for when the camera is rolling.

The weather can also be a challenge, especially when we're shooting outside in England! Sometimes it can be quite cold, and I might be wearing clothes that aren't very warm. Or if it's super sunny, the bright light can make it hard to keep my eyes open without squinting. I remember one outdoor shoot where it was so windy, and my hair kept flying everywhere! It was a bit tricky to keep everything looking just right. But you learn to adapt and just laugh it off. The teams are always careful to make sure I'm as comfortable as possible, bringing hot drinks or blankets if it's cold.

Another challenge, which can sometimes be tricky to handle, is the comments I see online. When my pictures go viral, especially the Gucci one, most people are incredibly kind and supportive. They send lovely messages saying how inspiring I am, or how beautiful the photos are. These comments make my heart so happy and remind me why I do what I do. But occasionally, there are people who say unkind things or who don't understand that everyone deserves to be celebrated. These comments can be mean or ignorant, saying things about my appearance or my abilities that aren't true or fair.

At first, seeing a negative comment used to make me feel a little sad or confused. I would think,

"Why would someone say that?" But my family has taught me to be strong and to remember that those words don't define me. My mum helps me to focus on the positive messages and to remember that my worth isn't determined by what a few people might say. It's like creating a bubble of love and positivity around myself and letting the unkind words bounce right off. I remind myself that my job is to spread joy and challenge old ideas, not to please everyone who sees my photos. It's impossible to make everyone happy, and that's okay!

It's important to understand that sometimes people say unkind things because they are scared, or they don't understand, or they might even be feeling unhappy themselves. It's not about me; it's about their own issues. I try to be the light and show them kindness, even if their words are not kind. My strength comes from within, and from the love of my family and friends.

Their belief in me is much stronger than any negative comment. So, instead of letting it make me feel small, I use that energy to make me even more determined to keep doing what I do, and keep shining brightly.

I also sometimes have to explain what Down syndrome means to people who might not understand. Many people have never met someone with Down syndrome before, and they might have questions or even some wrong ideas. I don't mind explaining, because it's an opportunity to educate and to help people learn. I like to show them that having Down syndrome is just a part of who I am, like having brown eyes or liking pop music. It doesn't stop me from living a full and exciting life, pursuing my dreams, and having fun.

Sometimes, people might underestimate me, or assume I can't do certain things because I have Down syndrome. For example, they might speak to me very slowly, or use very simple words, even when they don't need to. Or they might look to my mum for answers instead of talking directly to me. These moments can be a bit frustrating, but I try to handle them with patience and a smile. I show them, through my actions and my confidence, that I understand and that I am capable. I try to be a good example, showing that I'm capable, confident, and happy, just like anyone else. I've found that when people get to know me, their misunderstandings often disappear. It's all about connecting as people, not about differences.

One time, I was at an event, and someone asked me, "Ellie, what's it like to be different?" I paused for a moment, and then I smiled and said, "Everyone is different! That's what makes the world interesting." They looked surprised, and then they smiled too. It was a simple moment, but it felt powerful. It showed me that by being myself and speaking my truth, I can help people see things in a new way. Our differences are what make us unique and special, and that's something to celebrate, not to hide.

In life, just like in modelling, there will always be unexpected things that come up. It might be a difficult task, or a day when you just don't feel your best. But learning to face these challenges with a positive attitude, with resilience, and with the support of the people who love you, is so important. Every time I overcome a challenge, big or small, I feel stronger and more confident. It teaches me that I have inner strength that I can always rely on. It's about understanding that challenges are a part of life, and that you have the inner strength to overcome them, always keeping your head high and your smile bright. These experiences, even the tricky ones, help me grow.

Chapter 8: The Power of My Voice

As my modelling career grew, so did my platform. More and more people started to pay attention to my story, and I realised I had a wonderful opportunity to use my voice for good. It wasn't just about pretty pictures anymore; it was about speaking up for what I believe in, about standing up for a more inclusive world, and about inspiring others to be proud of who they are.

I've had the chance to do many interviews, both for big magazines and on television shows. It can be a little daunting sometimes, with bright lights, cameras, and microphones all around, and a lot of people watching! But I try to remember that I'm not just talking to the journalist; I'm sharing my message and my truth with everyone who is listening or reading. I love talking about how important it is for people with disabilities to be seen and represented in fashion and media. I believe that when everyone is included, the world becomes a richer, more vibrant place. It's like when you're drawing a picture, and you use all the colours in the crayon box, not just a few. The picture is much more beautiful and interesting when you use all the colours!

I remember my first big television interview. I was a bit nervous beforehand, my tummy felt a little fluttery. My mum helped me choose a nice outfit, and we went to the studio early. The TV hosts were very friendly and welcoming, and they made me feel comfortable. They asked me about my Gucci campaign, about how I started modelling, and about my dreams. I spoke from my heart, telling them how much I loved my job and how important it was to me to show the world that everyone is beautiful. When the interview was over, I felt a huge sense of relief and pride. It felt amazing to know that my words were reaching so many people.

One of the messages I love to share is about challenging stereotypes. What are stereotypes? They are like old, often untrue, ideas that some people have about groups of people. For example, a stereotype about people with Down syndrome might be that we can't do certain things, or that we all act the same way. But that's just not true! We are all individuals with unique talents, dreams, and personalities. Just like not all girls like the same colour, not all people with Down syndrome like the same things or have the same abilities. I want to show everyone that those old ideas are wrong!

I try to challenge these ideas just by being myself. By being a successful model, by speaking clearly in interviews, by showing my joy and confidence, I am proving that people with Down syndrome can achieve amazing things. I want to replace those old, untrue ideas with new, exciting ones where everyone is celebrated for who they are. I want to show that just because someone has a disability doesn't mean they can't achieve great things, or be models, or actors, or artists, or doctors, or anything else they set their minds to. I want to smash those old ideas and replace them with new, exciting ones where everyone is celebrated and given a chance to shine.

I also talk a lot about the importance of family and friends. My mum, dad, and sister have been my rock, my biggest supporters, and my best friends from day one. They always believed in me, even before I believed in myself. They taught me to be strong, to stand up for myself, and to always follow my dreams. When I feel happy, they celebrate with me. When I face a challenge, they are there to give me a hug and help me through it. They remind me that I am loved and that I can do anything.

Having a strong support system is so important when you're trying to achieve big things, or even just when you need a hug. My friends also make me laugh and feel loved. We share secrets, go shopping, and just have fun together. They treat me just like anyone else, and that's exactly how I want to be treated. Their friendship reminds me that I'm part of a wonderful community of people who care about me. It's like having a big, warm blanket of love and encouragement that wraps around you every day.

Using my voice also means being a role model. I get messages from parents and young girls who say that seeing me in campaigns or interviews makes them feel hopeful and proud. They say that I inspire them. That feeling is incredible, and it makes me want to keep working hard and keep being visible. It's a huge responsibility, but it's also a huge honour. I want to show everyone that if you embrace your uniqueness and work hard, you can achieve anything.

I've had the opportunity to speak at events and conferences, sometimes to big audiences. It's a chance to share my story directly and to connect with people. I talk about my journey, the power of believing in yourself, and the importance of diversity. I always try to be clear and confident, sharing my message from the heart. I believe that every person's voice has power, and when we all speak up for what is right and fair, we can make the world a better place. It's about creating a ripple effect of positivity and acceptance.

Chapter 9: Inspiring Others, Building a Future

One of the most rewarding parts of my journey has been seeing the impact my work has on others. When I get messages from parents saying my story has given them hope, or from young girls with Down syndrome saying they feel more confident because of me, it fills my heart with so much joy. It reminds me why I do what I do and how important it is to keep going. It's like throwing a little pebble into a pond and watching the ripples spread wider and wider. My pictures and my words are like those ripples, reaching out and hopefully making a positive difference in many lives.

I believe that every single person has the power to inspire others, no matter who they are or what they do. You don't have to be a model for a big brand or be on TV to make a difference. Sometimes, it's just about being kind to someone when they're feeling sad, or sharing your passions with enthusiasm, or showing courage in your everyday life when something feels a bit scary. Every act of bravery, every moment of self-belief, every time you share a genuine smile, can light up someone else's path. It's amazing how much good you can do just by being yourself and being positive.

I've had the chance to meet many young people and their families through my work, and these interactions are truly special. One time, after a photoshoot, a mum came up to me with her daughter, who was about your age and also had Down syndrome. The little girl had seen my pictures in a magazine, and her eyes were so bright when she looked at me. Her mum told me that seeing my work made her daughter feel like she could do anything, and it gave her mum so much hope for her daughter's future. We all shared a big hug, and it made me feel incredibly happy and proud. It's moments like these that mean the most to me, because they show me that my work is truly making a difference in real people's lives. It's not just about the glamour; it's about touching hearts.

I love hearing their stories – what their dreams are, what they love to do, and sometimes, the challenges they face. Sharing my own experiences helps them feel less alone, and seeing the smiles on their faces when they realize what's possible, that's the best feeling in the world. It makes me feel like we are all part of a big, supportive community, working together to make the world a more accepting place. We are all cheerleaders for each other! I want to continue to be a role model, to show that having Down syndrome is not a limitation, but just one part of a wonderful, unique identity. It's about celebrating every single person for their strengths and their own special sparkle.

Looking to the future, I have so many dreams! My head is bursting with exciting ideas. I want to continue modelling, of course, and to keep working with brands that truly believe in inclusivity and represent all kinds of people. I love the creativity of photoshoots, trying on new outfits, and working with talented teams. I hope to model for even more international brands and to see my face on billboards and in magazines all over the world. That would be amazing!

But I also want to explore acting more. You know how much I loved drama and plays when I was little? That passion is still very much alive! I would absolutely love to star in a movie or a TV show. Imagine being a character, telling a story, and making people feel emotions. That would be a fantastic new adventure. I've been taking acting classes, and it's a lot like modelling in some ways, because it's about expressing yourself and communicating without always using words. But it's also different because you get to become someone else entirely for a little while. I'm excited about the possibility of playing different roles and showing my versatility as an actress.

Beyond entertainment, I also want to keep using my voice to advocate for disability rights and to spread messages of self-love and acceptance. Advocating means speaking up for what is right and fair for people with disabilities. It means working to make sure everyone has equal opportunities and is treated with respect. I want to help make sure that people with Down syndrome are included in all parts of society – in schools, in workplaces, in sports, and in media. I believe that the more diverse faces we see in media, the more accepting and understanding society will become. When children grow up seeing all kinds of people in their books, on their TV shows, and in their magazines, it teaches them from a young age that everyone is valuable and belongs.

I dream of a future where no one feels left out because of who they are or how they were born. A future where differences are not just accepted, but celebrated as superpowers. I want to help build a world where every young girl, no matter her abilities or background, feels confident, loved, and knows that her dreams are possible. It's a big dream, but I truly believe we can get there, one step, one smile, and one brave voice at a time. I want to keep inspiring others to be proud of who they are, to chase their biggest dreams, and to always be kind. Every day, I try to live my life as an example of what's possible. My journey is continuing, and I can't wait to see what amazing things we can achieve together!

Chapter 10: My Message to You, My Future

You've journeyed with me through my story so far, from my early days of sparkle to my adventures in the fashion world and my passion for inspiring others. And now, as we reach the end of this book, I want to share some of the most important lessons I've learned with you, my wonderful reader. These aren't just lessons for models or famous people; they're lessons for everyone, because every single one of you has a unique and important story to tell.

The very first thing I want you to remember is this: **You are beautiful, just the way you are.** This isn't just about what you look like on the outside, although every single one of us has our own unique beauty. It's about the beauty inside you – your kind heart, your bright ideas, your amazing sense of humor, and your sparkling personality. Your smile, your laughter, your unique talents, and even your quirks – these are all parts of what make you incredibly special and wonderful. Don't ever, ever let anyone tell you that you're not enough, or that you need to change to fit into someone else's idea of perfect. There is no 'perfect' way to be a person, only your own amazing way.

For me, embracing my own beauty includes having Down syndrome. It's a part of who I am, and it has given me a special way of seeing the world and connecting with people. It makes me unique, and that's a good thing! Think about what makes you special. Maybe you're really good at art, or super speedy at running, or you're an amazing storyteller. Maybe you have a laugh that makes everyone happy, or you're incredibly thoughtful. These are all parts of your unique sparkle. Find your own special something and celebrate it loudly! Practice looking in the mirror and telling yourself something kind and positive every day. It might feel silly at first, but it really helps build that self-love. Remember, true beauty shines from within, and when you love yourself, that light radiates out to the world.

Secondly, I want to talk about **dreams and bravery.** Everyone has dreams, big and small. Maybe you dream of being an artist, a scientist, a dancer, a fantastic baker, an astronaut, or even a princess! Whatever your dream is, no matter how big or small it seems right now, hold onto it tightly in your heart. Give it room to grow.

It takes courage to pursue your dreams, especially when they seem difficult, or when others might not understand them, or even tell you that you can't do it. But remember, little steps add up to big journeys. My journey to becoming a model started with a love for performing and a brave decision to try something new, even when I was a bit nervous. There will be times when things get tough, or when you feel like giving up. That's when you need to be extra brave. Take a deep breath, remember your dream, and take one more small step forward. Be brave enough to try, brave enough to learn from your mistakes, and brave enough to keep going, even if you face setbacks. Every time you try something new, or push past a fear, you become a little bit braver, and that bravery will help you with everything in life. My mum always says, "Ellie, if you never try, you'll never know!" and that always encourages me.

Thirdly, remember the **power of kindness and connection.** The world is a much, much better place when we are kind to each other. Kindness starts with how you treat yourself – speak kindly to yourself, forgive yourself when you make mistakes, and celebrate your own successes. Then, extend that kindness to your family, your friends, and everyone you meet, even strangers. A simple smile, a helping hand, or a kind word can make a huge difference to someone's day.

Think about how good it feels when someone is kind to you. You can give that feeling to others! Listen to others, try to understand their perspectives, even if they see things differently than you. Always offer a helping hand if you can, whether it's helping a friend with their homework, or holding a door open for someone. Having strong connections with people who love and support you is one of the greatest treasures in life. My family and friends have been my guiding stars; their love and support have made me strong and confident. Cherish those relationships, spend time with the people who make you feel good, and be a good friend in return. Remember, kindness is a superpower that makes the world brighter for everyone.

And finally, never forget that **your voice matters.** Your voice is important, and it deserves to be heard. Whether it's a quiet whisper of encouragement to a friend who is feeling shy, or speaking up in class about an idea you have, or standing up for someone who is being treated unfairly, your words have power. Use your voice to spread positivity, to advocate for fairness and inclusion, and to share your unique story.

My journey has shown me how much impact one person's voice can have. When I share my story, I hope it helps people understand that diversity is beautiful and that everyone belongs. You don't have to be on TV to make your voice count. You can use your voice in your family, in your school, in your local community. Share your ideas, ask questions, and tell people what you believe in. You have the ability to inspire others, just by being authentically you and speaking your truth. Don't be afraid to be heard. The world needs your unique perspective, your kindness, and your dreams.

This chapter is my personal message to you, a warm embrace of encouragement and belief. I want you to know that you have everything you need inside you to live a life full of purpose, happiness, and incredible impact. Go out there and shine brightly, just like the star you are! And remember, your story is just beginning, and it's going to be an amazing one. The world is waiting for your sparkle!

Afterword: A Radiant Force for Change

You have now journeyed through the inspiring life of Ellie Goldstein, a young woman who has defied expectations and illuminated the global stage with her unique beauty and unwavering spirit. From her joyful beginnings in East London to her groundbreaking campaigns for world-renowned brands, Ellie's story is a powerful testament to the impact one individual can have in shaping a more inclusive world.

Ellie's early life, nurtured by a loving and supportive family, provided the foundation for her incredible journey. They fostered her natural talents and encouraged her to embrace every opportunity, instilling in her the self-belief that would become her hallmark. Her inherent passion for performing and her vibrant personality set her on a path where she would eventually captivate audiences and challenge pre-conceived notions of beauty.

Her collaboration with Zebedee Management marked a pivotal moment, connecting her with an agency that champions diversity and sees potential where others might have overlooked it. It was through this partnership that Ellie's talent for modelling truly blossomed, leading to the iconic Gucci Beauty campaign that propelled her into the international spotlight. Her radiant image, a powerful symbol of authentic beauty, resonated across the globe, sparking conversations and inspiring countless individuals.

Ellie's impact extends far beyond the glossy pages of magazines. She has become a vital voice for inclusivity, advocating for better representation of people with disabilities in media and fashion. Through her interviews and public engagements, she eloquently shares her experiences, encourages self-love, and challenges the stereotypes that have long limited opportunities for individuals with Down syndrome. Her message is clear: difference is not a barrier; it is a celebrated strength.

Throughout her career, Ellie has faced challenges, from the demanding nature of professional photoshoots to the occasional unkindness of online comments. Yet, with a calm determination and an ever-present smile, she has navigated these moments, demonstrating remarkable resilience. Her ability to remain focused on her positive impact and the love from her supporters is a powerful lesson in inner strength.

Beyond her professional achievements, Ellie remains a vibrant young woman with diverse passions. Her love for dancing, art, and cherished time with family and friends highlights the importance of a balanced life, where personal joy and connection nourish the spirit. These aspects of her life reinforce the message that living fully and authentically is key to true happiness and well-being.

Ellie Goldstein's legacy is still being written, but already, she stands as a beacon of hope and an agent of change. Her life teaches us that true beauty emanates from confidence, kindness, and the courage to be oneself. She reminds us that every person has inherent worth and the potential to achieve extraordinary things. Her "Her-story" encourages young girls everywhere to embrace their unique identities, pursue their dreams with passion, and understand that their unique sparkle can indeed light up the world, making it a more vibrant, accepting, and beautiful place for everyone.

Quiz Time!

1. Where in London was Ellie Goldstein born?

2. What is the name of Ellie's mother and father?

3. Besides her parents, who else is mentioned as one of Ellie's biggest cheerleaders?

4. In school, what were Ellie's favorite subjects?

5. What did Ellie use as a pretend microphone when she was a child?

6. What is the name of the special agency that Ellie joined?

7. In what year was Ellie chosen to be part of the Gucci Beauty campaign?

8. What was the name of the photographer for the Gucci Beauty campaign?

9. What is one of Ellie's biggest passions outside of modeling that involves movement and music?

10. What does the book state is the meaning behind the name of the book series, **herStory**?

Answers

1. Ellie Goldstein was born in Ilford, East London.
2. Her mother's name is Yvonne, and her father's name is Mark.
3. Her sister, Amy, is also mentioned as one of her biggest cheerleaders.
4. Her favorite subjects were anything creative, such as art, music, and drama.
5. She used a hairbrush as a pretend microphone.
6. She joined an agency called Zebedee Management.
7. Ellie's first big break with the Gucci Beauty campaign was in 2020.
8. The photographer for the campaign was David PD Hyde.
9. Dancing is one of her biggest passions.
10. The book states that **herStory** invites readers on a journey told directly by inspiring women and brings a legendary woman to life in her own words.

herStory
inspirational women for girls

Who will inspire you next?

Did model, Ellie Goldstein's story inspire you?

Look out for other fearless females in the **herStory** series!

Scan Me for More herStories!

Printed in Dunstable, United Kingdom